AS WE BELIEVE SO WE PRAY

Brian Mayne

As We Believe
So We Pray

A BOOK OF DAILY PRAYER

colUMBA

First published in 2003 by
THE COLUMBA PRESS
55a Spruce Avenue, Stillorgan Industrial Park,
Blackrock, Co Dublin, Ireland

Designed by Bill Bolger
Cross on the cover is from a 7th century grave stone
from Saul Parish, worked in stitching by Felix
Blennerhassett, Dublin.
Origination by The Columba Press
Printed in Ireland by ColourBooks Ltd, Dublin

ISBN 1 85607 416 1

Contents

Introduction

In the new edition of the Church of Ireland Book of Common Prayer a skeleton framework of a simple form of daily prayer is given.

This book offers fifteen workings out of that framework. They are intended to help busy people to pray. Based on phrases from the Apostles' Creed, Forms 1 to 12 may be used on weekdays for a fortnight. At certain seasons particular forms may be used more extensively over a week or more.

At other times people may like to use a particular form more frequently so that the rhythm of prayer may, as it were, become part of oneself.

Form 13 may be used to remember the saints and others into whose heritage twenty-first century disciples have entered. A list of commemorations is given with the Calendar in the Book of Common Prayer.

Form 14 may be used in thanksgiving and preparation for Holy Communion perhaps on a Saturday evening.

Form 15 may be used in times of sickness or when praying for the sick

The choice of psalm and reading may be from the appointed weekday lectionary or from some other system of regular bible reading. The short readings given here are for convenience when a bible is not to hand.

Psalm refrains give a context to the psalm and may be repeated between verses or at the beginning and end of the psalm only.

Daily Prayer: A Simple Structure

FROM THE BOOK OF COMMON PRAYER
OF THE CHURCH OF IRELAND

This reflects the way the Church structures its common prayer and may be a basis for personal or family devotions

Preparation

A SENTENCE OF SCRIPTURE

A PRAYER OF PENITENCE

PRAISE

The Word of God

A PSALM

A BIBLE READING

A CANTICLE

Prayer

INTERCESSIONS AND THANKSGIVINGS

THE COLLECT OF THE DAY
or another collect

THE LORD'S PRAYER

AN ENDING

The choice of psalm and reading may be from the appointed weekday lectionary or from some other system of regular bible reading.

Form 1   The Father Almighty

Preparation

A SENTENCE OF SCRIPTURE

Jesus said: whenever you pray, go into your room and
shut the door and pray to your Father who is in secret;
and your Father who sees in secret will reward you.
Matthew 6: 6

A PRAYER OF PENITENCE

O God, our loving Father in heaven,
we confess that we have sinned against you;
we have broken your commandments;
we have often been selfish,
and we have not loved you as we should.
For these, and all our sins, forgive us we pray;
through our Lord and Saviour Jesus Christ. Amen.

PRAISE

Dear Lord and Father of mankind,
Forgive our foolish ways;
Re-clothe us in our rightful mind,
In purer lives thy service find,
In deeper reverence, praise.

Drop thy still dews of quietness,
Till all our strivings cease:
Take from our souls the strain and stress,
And let our ordered lives confess
The beauty of thy peace.

Breathe through the heats of our desire
Thy coolness and thy balm;
Let sense be dumb, let flesh retire;
Speak through the earthquake, wind and fire,
O still small voice of calm.

The Word of God

Refrain:
We are the people of his pasture,
and the sheep of his hand.

1   The Lord is my shepherd;
    therefore can I lack nothing.
2   He makes me lie down in green pastures
    and leads me beside still waters.
3   He shall refresh my soul
    and guide me in the paths of righteousness for
        his name's sake.
4   Though I walk through the valley of the shadow of
        death,
    I will fear no evil;
    for you are with me;
    your rod and your staff, they comfort me.
5   You spread a table before me
    in the presence of those who trouble me;
    you have anointed my head with oil and my cup
        shall be full.
6   Surely goodness and loving mercy shall follow me
        all the days of my life,
    and I will dwell in the house of the Lord for ever.

A BIBLE READING

Philip said to Jesus, 'Lord, show us the Father, and we
will be satisfied.' Jesus said to him, 'Have I been with
you all this time, Philip, and you still do not know me?
Whoever has seen me has seen the Father. How can
you say, 'Show us the Father'? Do you not believe that
I am in the Father and the Father is in me? The words
that I say to you I do not speak on my own; but the

Father who dwells in me does his works. Believe me that I am in the Father and the Father is in me; but if you do not, then believe me because of the works themselves. Very truly, I tell you, the one who believes in me will also do the works that I do and, in fact, will do greater works than these, because I am going to the Father.' *John 14: 8-12*

Te Deum Part 1

1   We praise you, O God
    we acclaim you as the Lord;
2   All creation worships you
    the Father everlasting.
3   To you all angels, all the powers of heaven
    the cherubim and seraphim, sing in endless praise,
4   Holy, holy, holy Lord, God of power and might
    heaven and earth are full of your glory.
5   The glorious company of apostles praise you
    the noble fellowship of prophets praise you.
6   The white-robed army of martyrs praise you
    throughout the world, the holy Church acclaims
        you.
7   Father, of majesty unbounded
    your true and only Son, worthy of all praise,
    the Holy Spirit, advocate and guide.

Prayer

Give thanks for Christ's revelation of our Father in heaven,
for the power to become children of God.

Pray for home and family life,
for children deprived of homes,
for relationships in daily life and work.

or this prayer:
Father in heaven,
your Son has taught us to call you our Father
and by his life and death has enabled us to become
your children:
In obedient lives may we grow in love for you
and show that love by seeking the good of all our brothers and sisters;
through Jesus Christ our Lord. Amen.

Abba, Father,
you know me,
you love me,
you have a use for me now and for ever. Amen.

Form 2   Maker of heaven and earth

Preparation

A SENTENCE OF SCRIPTURE

O Lord, how manifold are your works! In wisdom you
have made them all. *Psalm 104: 24*

A PRAYER OF PENITENCE

The Lord is merciful and gracious.
Lord, have mercy.

Great is his steadfast love towards those who fear him.
Christ, have mercy.

The Lord knows how we were made, he remembers
that we are dust.
Lord, have mercy.

PRAISE

Immortal, invisible, God only wise,
In light inaccessible hid from our eyes,
Most blessed, Most glorious, the Ancient of Days,
Almighty, victorious, thy great name we praise.

Unresting, unhasting, and silent as light,
Nor wanting, nor wasting, thou rulest in might;
Thy justice like mountains high soaring above
Thy clouds which are fountains of goodness and love.

To all, life thou givest, to both great and small;
In all life thou livest, the true life of all;
We blossom and flourish as leaves on the tree,
And wither and perish; but naught changeth thee.

Great Father of glory, pure Father of light,
Thine angels adore thee, all veiling their sight;
All laud we would render: O help us to see
'Tis only the splendour of light hideth thee.

The Word of God

PSALM 100

Refrain:
Rejoice in the Lord, you righteous,
and give thanks to his holy name.

1   O be joyful in the Lord, all the earth;
    serve the Lord with gladness and come before
        his presence with a song.

2   Know that the Lord is God;
    it is he that has made us and we are his;
    we are his people and the sheep of his pasture.

3   Enter his gates with thanksgiving and his courts
    with praise;
    give thanks to him and bless his name.

4   For the Lord is gracious; his steadfast love is
        everlasting,
    and his faithfulness endures from generation to
        generation.

A BIBLE READING

The God who made the world and everything in it, he who is Lord of heaven and earth, does not live in shrines made by human hands, nor is he served by human hands, as though he needed anything, since he himself gives to all mortals life and breath and all things. From one ancestor he made all nations to inhabit the whole earth, and he allotted the times of their existence and the boundaries of the places where they would live, so that they would search for God and perhaps grope for him and find him – though indeed he is not far from each one of us. For 'In him we live and move and have our being'.

Acts 17: 24-28

Bless the Lord (Song of the Three 29-34)

1   Bless the Lord the God of our fathers
     sing his praise and exalt him for ever.
2   Bless his holy and glorious name
     sing his praise and exalt him for ever.
3   Bless him in his holy and glorious temple
     sing his praise and exalt him for ever.
4   Bless him who beholds the depths
     sing his praise and exalt him for ever.
5   Bless him seated between the cherubim
     sing his praise and exalt him for ever.
6   Bless him on the throne of his kingdom
     sing his praise and exalt him for ever.
7   Bless him in the heights of heaven
     sing his praise and exalt him for ever.
8   Bless the Father the Son and the Holy Spirit
     sing his praise and exalt him for ever.

Prayer

INTERCESSIONS AND THANKSGIVINGS

Pray for the world,
    for right use of creation,
    for scientists and all who seek to extend human
    knowledge,
    for our responsibility in our everyday living.

Give thanks for the wonders of creation
    for all that is good in men and women made in
    God's image

or this prayer:
Eternal God and Father,
you create us by your power and redeem us by your
love:
Guide and strengthen us by your Spirit,
that we may give ourselves in love and service
to you and to one another;
through Jesus Christ our Lord. Amen.

THE LORD'S PRAYER

AN ENDING

God,
Creator, Redeemer and Strengthgiver,
be with us today and always. Amen.

Form 3   Jesus Christ, our Lord

Preparation

A SENTENCE OF SCRIPTURE

Jesus said to the disciples : 'Who do you say I am?'
Simon Peter answered: 'You are the Messiah, the Son
of the living God!' *Matthew 16: 15-16*

A PRAYER OF PENITENCE

Jesus Christ, Master and Lord:
We come in sorrow for our sins,
and confess to you our weakness and unbelief.
We have sought to live by our own strength,
by the light of our own eyes
and for this world alone.
In your mercy forgive us.
Lord, hear us and help us;
for your mercy's sake. Amen.

PRAISE

At the Name of Jesus
Every knee shall bow,
Every tongue confess him
King of glory now;
'Tis the Father's pleasure
We should call him Lord,
Who from the beginning
Was the mighty Word.

Mighty and mysterious
In the highest height,
God from everlasting,
Very Light of Light;

In the Father's bosom
With the Spirit blest,
Love, in Love eternal,
Rest in perfect rest.

Name him, brothers, name him,
With love as strong as death,
But with awe and wonder,
And with bated breath;
He is God the Saviour,
He is Christ the Lord,
Ever to be worshipped,
Trusted and adored.

The Word of God   PSALM 8

Refrain:
You are great and do wonderful things,
you alone are God.

1   O Lord our governor,
    how glorious is your name in all the world!
2   Your majesty above the heavens is praised
    out of the mouths of babes at the breast.
3   You have founded a stronghold against your foes,
    that you might still the enemy and the avenger.
4   When I consider your heavens, the work of
        your fingers,
    the moon and the stars that you have ordained,
5   What is man, that you should be mindful of him;
    the son of man, that you should seek him out?
6   You have made him little lower than the angels
    and crown him with glory and honour.
7   You have given him dominion over the works of
        your hands
    and put all things under his feet,
8   All sheep and oxen,

even the wild beasts of the field,
the birds of the air, the fish of the sea
and whatsoever moves in the paths of the sea.
9 O Lord our governor,
how glorious is your name in all the world!

A BIBLE READING

Christ is the image of the invisible God, the firstborn of
all creation; for in him all things in heaven and on earth
were created, things visible and invisible, whether
thrones or dominions or rulers or powers – all things
have been created through him and for him. He himself is before all things, and in him all things hold
together. He is the head of the body, the church; he is
the beginning, the firstborn from the dead, so that he
might come to have first place in everything. For in
him all the fullness of God was pleased to dwell, and
through him God was pleased to reconcile to himself
all things, whether on earth or in heaven, by making
peace through the blood of his cross.
Colossians 1: 13-20

A CANTICLE

Te Deum Part 2
8 You, Christ, are the King of glory
the eternal Son of the Father.
9 When you took our flesh to set us free
you humbly chose the virgin's womb.
10 You overcame the sting of death
and opened the kingdom of heaven to all believers.
11 You are seated at God's right hand in glory:
we believe that you will come to be our judge.
12 Come then, Lord, and help your people,
bought with the price of your own blood
and bring us with your saints to glory everlasting.

Prayer

Pray for people in every part of the world
> *those who work ...*
> *the unemployed ...*
> *those in education ...*
> *those in communications ...*
> *those who maintain the life of the community ...*

Give thanks
> *for Christ's care for people,*
> *and his joy in obedience ...*
> *for the value he gave to human labour,*
> *the strength he promised us for service,*
> *the call to follow in his way ...*

THE COLLECT OF THE DAY

or this prayer:
Lord Jesus Christ,
we thank you for all the benefits you have won for us,
for all the pains and insults you have borne for us.
Most merciful redeemer, friend and brother,
may we know you more clearly,
love you more dearly,
and follow you more nearly,
day by day. Amen.

THE LORD'S PRAYER

AN ENDING

The grace of our Lord Jesus Christ,
and the love of God,
and the fellowship of the Holy Spirit,
be with us all evermore. Amen.

Form 4   Born of the Virgin Mary

Preparation

A child has been born for us, a son given to us; authority rests upon his shoulders; and he is named Wonderful Counsellor, Mighty God, Everlasting Father, Prince of Peace. *Isaiah 9: 6*

A PRAYER OF PENITENCE

God, you loved the world so much
that you sent your Son to be our Saviour:
we confess that we have sinned against you;
we ask you to forgive us for his sake
and to make us holy to serve you in the world:
through Jesus Christ our Lord. Amen.

PRAISE

Child in the manger,
Infant of Mary;
Outcast and stranger,
Lord of all!
Child who inherits
All our transgressions,
All our demerits
On him fall.

Once the most holy
Child of salvation,
Gentle and lowly,
Lived below;
Now, as our glorious
Mighty Redeemer,
See him victorious
O'er each foe.

Prophets foretold him,
Infant of wonder;
Angels behold him
On his throne;
Worthy our Saviour
Of all their praises;
Happy for ever
Are his own.

The Word of God

PSALM 85

Refrain:
Show us your mercy, O Lord,
and grant us your salvation.

8 I will listen to what the Lord God will say,
    for he shall speak peace to his people and to the
      faithful,
    that they turn not again to folly.

9 Truly, his salvation is near to those who fear him,
    that his glory may dwell in our land.

10 Mercy and truth are met together,
    righteousness and peace have kissed each other;

11 Truth shall spring up from the earth
    and righteousness look down from heaven.

12 The Lord will indeed give all that is good,
    and our land will yield its increase.

13 Righteousness shall go before him
    and direct his steps in the way.

A BIBLE READING

In those days a decree went out from Emperor
Augustus that all the world should be registered. This
was the first registration and was taken while Quirinius

was governor of Syria. All went to their own towns to be registered. Joseph also went from the town of Nazareth in Galilee to Judea, to the city of David called Bethlehem, because he was descended from the house and family of David. He went to be registered with Mary, to whom he was engaged and who was expecting a child. While they were there, the time came for her to deliver her child. And she gave birth to her firstborn son and wrapped him in bands of cloth, and laid him in a manger, because there was no place for them in the inn.

Luke 2: 1-7

A CANTICLE

Magnificat

1   My soul proclaims the greatness of the Lord:
    my spirit rejoices in God my Saviour.

2   Who has looked with favour on his lowly servant:
    from this day all generations will call me blessed

3   The Almighty has done great things for me:
    and holy is his name.

4   God has mercy on those who fear him:
    from generation to generation.

5   The Lord has shown strength with his arm:
    and scattered the proud in their conceit.

6   Casting down the mighty from their thrones:
    and lifting up the lowly.

7   God has filled the hungry with good things:
    and sent the rich away empty.

8   He has come to the aid of his servant Israel:
    to remember the promise of mercy,

9   The promise made to our forebears:
    to Abraham and his children for ever.

Prayer

Pray for
> *homes and families*
> *friends, relations and neighbours ...*
> *relationships in daily life and work ...*
> *those who are estranged ...*
> *those who feel unloved ...*
> *all ministries of care ...*

Give thanks for the joy of loving and being loved
> *for friendship,*
> *the lives to which our own are bound,*
> *the gift of peace with God and with one another.*

THE COLLECT OF THE DAY

or this prayer:
Almighty God,
who wonderfully created us in your own image
and yet more wonderfully restored us
through your Son Jesus Christ:
Grant that, as he came to share in our humanity,
so we may share the life of his divinity;
who is alive and reigns with you and the Holy Spirit,
one God, now and for ever. Amen.

THE LORD'S PRAYER

AN ENDING

May he, who by his incarnation gathered into one
all things earthly and heavenly,
fill us with his joy and peace Amen.

Form 5   Crucified ... dead and buried

Preparation

May I never boast of anything except the cross of our
Lord Jesus Christ, by which the world has been crucified to me, and I to the world. *Galatians 6: 14*

A PRAYER OF PENITENCE

Lord Jesus Christ,
Son of God,
have mercy on me, a sinner.
This prayer may be repeated several times slowly.

PRAISE

There is a green hill far away,
Without a city wall,
Where the dear Lord was crucified,
Who died to save us all.

We may not know, we cannot tell
What pains he had to bear,
But we believe it was for us
He hung and suffered there.

He died that we might be forgiven,
he died to make us good,
That we might go at last to heaven,
Saved by his precious Blood.

There was no other good enough
To pay the price of sin,
He only could unlock the gate
Of heaven, and let us in.

Oh! dearly, dearly has he loved,
And we must love him too,
And trust in his redeeming Blood,
And try his works to do.

The Word of God

PSALM 22

Refrain:
O Lord, you are my strength, hasten to help me.

1   My God, my God, why have you forsaken me,
    and are so far from my salvation,
    from the words of my distress?

2   O my God, I cry in the daytime,
        but you do not answer;
    and by night also, but I find no rest.

3   Yet you are the Holy One,
    enthroned upon the praises of Israel.

4   Our forebears trusted in you;
    they trusted, and you delivered them.

5   They cried out to you and were delivered;
    they put their trust in you
        and were not confounded.

6   But as for me, I am a worm and no man,
    scorned by all and despised by the people.

7   All who see me laugh me to scorn;
    they curl their lips and wag their heads, saying,

8   'He trusted in the Lord; let him deliver him;
    let him deliver him, if he delights in him.'

9   But it is you that took me out of the womb
    and laid me safe upon my mother's breast.

10 On you was I cast ever since I was born;
    you are my God even from my mother's womb.

11 Be not far from me, for trouble is near at hand
    and there is none to help.

A BIBLE READING

When it was noon, darkness came over the whole land
until three in the afternoon. At three o'clock Jesus cried
out with a loud voice, 'Eloi, Eloi, lema sabachthani?'
which means, 'My God, my God, why have you forsak-
en me?' When some of the bystanders heard it, they
said, 'Listen, he is calling for Elijah.' And someone ran,
filled a sponge with sour wine, put it on a stick, and
gave it to him to drink, saying, 'Wait, let us see whether
Elijah will come to take him down.' Then Jesus gave a
loud cry and breathed his last. And the curtain of the
temple was torn in two, from top to bottom. Now when
the centurion, who stood facing him, saw that in this
way he breathed his last, he said, 'Truly this man was
God's Son!' *Mark 15: 33-39*

A CANTICLE

Saviour of the World

1   Jesus Saviour of the world, come to us in your mercy:
    we look to you to save and help us.
2   By your cross and your life laid down, you set your
        people free:
    we look to you to save and help us.
3   When they were ready to perish you saved your
        disciples:
    we look to you to come to our help.
4   In the greatness of your mercy loose us from our
        chains:
    forgive the sins of all your people.
5   Make yourself known as our Saviour and mighty
        Deliverer:
    save and help us that we may praise you.
6   Come now and dwell with us Lord Christ Jesus,
    hear our prayer and be with us always.

7   And when you come in your glory
    make us to be one with you
    and to share the life of your kingdom. Amen.

Prayer

INTERCESSIONS AND THANKSGIVINGS

Pray for all who suffer
*   the hungry*
*   refugees*
*   prisoners*
*   all who bring sin and suffering to others.*

Give thanks for
*   the Cross of Christ at the heart of creation,*
*   the assurance that God's mercy knows no limit*
*   for all ministries of healing*
*   and all that sets people free from pain and fear.*

THE COLLECT OF THE DAY

or this prayer:
Almighty and everlasting God,
who in your tender love towards the human race
sent your Son our Saviour Jesus Christ
to take upon him our flesh
and to suffer death upon the cross:
Grant that we may follow the example
of his patience and humility,
and also be made partakers of his resurrection;
through Jesus Christ our Lord. Amen.

THE LORD'S PRAYER

AN ENDING

Saviour of the world,
by your Cross and precious Blood, you have redeemed us:
Save us and help us, O Lord, we pray. Amen.

28   *Crucified ... dead and buried*

Form 6   On the third day he rose again

Preparation

A SENTENCE OF SCRIPTURE

If we have died with Christ, we believe that we shall also live with him. *Romans 6: 8*

A PRAYER OF PENITENCE

Almighty God,
in raising Jesus from the grave,
you shattered the power of sin and death.
We confess that we remain captive to doubt and fear.
We have sinned in disobeying your commandments.
Forgive us, God of mercy.
Help us to trust your power to change and renew us.
Forgiven may we know the joy of life abundant
given us in Jesus Christ, the risen Lord. Amen.

PRAISE

Thine be the glory, risen, conquering Son,
endless is the victory thou o'er death hast won;
angels in bright raiment rolled the stone away,
kept the folded grave-clothes where thy body lay:
> *Thine be the glory, risen, conquering Son,*
> *endless is the victory thou o'er death hast won.*

Lo, Jesus meets us, risen from the tomb;
lovingly he greets us, scatters fear and gloom;
let the Church with gladness hymns of triumph sing,
for her Lord now liveth, death hath lost its sting:

No more we doubt thee, glorious Prince of Life;
life is nought without thee: aid us in our strife;
make us more than conquerors through thy deathless love;
bring us safe through Jordan to thy home above.

The Word of God

Refrain:
You will show me the path of life,
in your presence is the fullness of joy.

14 The Lord is my strength and my song,
    and he has become my salvation.

15 Joyful shouts of salvation
    sound from the tents of the righteous:

16 'The right hand of the Lord does mighty deeds;
    the right hand of the Lord raises up;
    the right hand of the Lord does mighty deeds.'

17 I shall not die, but live
    and declare the works of the Lord.

18 The Lord has punished me sorely,
    but he has not given me over to death.

19 Open to me the gates of righteousness,
    that I may enter and give thanks to the Lord.

20 This is the gate of the Lord;
    the righteous shall enter through it.

21 I will give thanks to you, for you have answered me
    and have become my salvation.

22 The stone which the builders rejected
    has become the chief cornerstone.

23 This is the Lord's doing,
    and it is marvellous in our eyes.

24 This is the day that the Lord has made;
    we will rejoice and be glad in it.

A BIBLE READING

Now I would remind you, brothers and sisters, of the
good news that I proclaimed to you, which you in turn
received, in which also you stand, through which also

On the third day he rose again

you are being saved, if you hold firmly to the message that I proclaimed to you – unless you have come to believe in vain. For I handed on to you as of first importance what I in turn had received: that Christ died for our sins in accordance with the scriptures, and that he was buried, and that he was raised on the third day in accordance with the scriptures, and that he appeared to Cephas, then to the twelve. Then he appeared to more than five hundred brothers and sisters at one time, most of whom are still alive, though some have died. Then he appeared to James, then to all the apostles. Last of all, as to one untimely born, he appeared also to me. *1 Corinthians 15: 1-8*

A CANTICLE

Easter Anthems

1   Christ our passover has been sacrificed for us:
    therefore let us celebrate the feast.

2   Not with the old leaven of corruption and
        wickedness,
    but with the unleavened bread of sincerity and truth.

3   Christ once raised from the dead dies no more:
    death has no more dominion over him.

4   In dying, he died to sin once for all:
    in living, he lives to God.

5   See yourselves therefore as dead to sin,
    and alive to God in Jesus Christ our Lord.

6   Christ has been raised from the dead,
    the first fruits of those who sleep.

7   For as by man came death,
    by man has come also the resurrection of the dead.

8   For as in Adam all die,
    even so in Christ shall all be made alive.

Prayer

Pray for

all who called to proclaim the Easter message
all clergy and ministers of the Gospel
all who mourn
those who find faith in the Risen Jesus difficult.

Give thanks for

the Glorious Resurrection
the Easter hope that we will rise with him
for all our foretaste of eternal life through
baptism and the eucharist.

THE COLLECT OF THE DAY

or this prayer:

Lord of all life and power,
who through the mighty resurrection of your Son
overcame the old order of sin and death
to make all things new in him:
Grant that we, being dead to sin
and alive to you in Jesus Christ,
may reign with him in glory;
to whom with you and the Holy Spirit
be praise and honour, glory and might,
now and in all eternity. Amen.

THE LORD'S PRAYER

AN ENDING

Lord Jesus,
make us a people
whose song is alleluia,
whose sign is peace
and whose name is love.
and you are all in all. Amen.

Form 7   Ascended into heaven

Preparation

A SENTENCE OF SCRIPTURE

If we have died with Christ, we believe that we shall
also live with him. *Romans 6: 8*

A PRAYER OF PENITENCE

Have mercy on us, O God, the Almighty,
Jesus Christ, Son of the living God;
Eternal Judge, have mercy.
Royal abundant Lord,
Great God, to whom we pray, have mercy,
for it is your very nature to have mercy and to forgive;
thanks be to God.

PRAISE

Lord, enthroned in heavenly splendour,
First begotten from the dead,
Thou alone, our strong Defender,
Liftest up thy people's head.
Alleluia, alleluia,
Jesu, true and living Bread.

Paschal Lamb, thine Offering finished
Once for all when thou wast slain,
In its fulness undiminished
Shall for evermore remain,
Alleluia, alleluia,
Cleansing souls from every stain.

Great High Priest of our profession,
Through the veil thou wentest in,
By thy mighty intercession
Grace and peace for us to win;
Alleluia, alleluia,
Only sacrifice for sin.

Life-imparting, heavenly Manna,
Smitten rock with streaming side,
Heaven and earth with one Hosanna,
Worship thee, the Lamb that died,
Alleluia, alleluia,
Risen, ascended, glorified!

The Word of God

Refrain:
The Lord is king, the Lord has put on his glory
and girded himself with strength.

1   Clap your hands together, all you peoples;
      O sing to God with shouts of joy.

2   For the Lord Most High is to be feared;
      he is the great King over all the earth.

3   He subdued the peoples under us
      and the nations under our feet.
      He has chosen our heritage for us,
      the pride of Jacob, whom he loves.

5   God has gone up with a merry noise,
      the Lord with the sound of the trumpet.

6   O sing praises to God, sing praises;
      sing praises to our King, sing praises.

7   For God is the King of all the earth;
      sing praises with all your skill.

8   God reigns over the nations;
      God has taken his seat upon his holy throne.

9   The nobles of the peoples are gathered together
      with the people of the God of Abraham.

10 For the powers of the earth belong to God
      and he is very highly exalted.

I pray that the God of our Lord Jesus Christ, the Father of glory, may give you a spirit of wisdom and revelation as you come to know him, so that, with the eyes of your heart enlightened, you may know what is the hope to which he has called you, what are the riches of his glorious inheritance among the saints, and what is the immeasurable greatness of his power for us who believe, according to the working of his great power. God put this power to work in Christ when he raised him from the dead and seated him at his right hand in the heavenly places, far above all rule and authority and power and dominion, and above every name that is named, not only in this age but also in the age to come. And he has put all things under his feet and has made him the head over all things for the church, which is his body, the fullness of him who fills all in all.

Ephesians 1: 17-23

A Song of Christ's Glory

1 Christ Jesus was in the form of God;
   but he did not cling to equality with God.
2 He emptied himself, taking the form of a servant
   and was born in our human likeness.
3 And being found in human form he humbled
        himself
   and became obedient unto death even death on a cross.
4 Therefore God has highly exalted him:
   and bestowed on him the name above every name.
5 That at the name of Jesus every knee should bow:
   in heaven and on earth and under the earth.
6 And every tongue confess that Jesus Christ is Lord:
   to the glory of God the Father.

Prayer

Pray for
> the nations of the world and their leaders,
> for peace and the reconciliation of all,
> where differences divide men and women.

Give thanks for
> the apostolic gospel committed to the church,
> for all works of compassion,
> for every service that proclaims God's love.

THE COLLECT OF THE DAY

or this prayer:
Risen and ascended Lord,
you have promised to be with us always
to the end of time itself:
Teach us to be aware of your presence
and to abide in your love,
that we may walk in the way that leads to glory,
where you live and reign
with the Father and the Holy Spirit,
one God, now and for ever. Amen.

THE LORD'S PRAYER

AN ENDING

Christ has opened the gate of glory;
Christ prays for us at the right hand of the Father.
Christ descended to lift us up to be with him.
Alleluia!

Form 8   He will come again

Preparation

A SENTENCE OF SCRIPTURE

Jesus said, 'About that day and hour no one knows, nei-
ther the angels in heaven, nor the Son, but only the
Father. Beware, keep alert for you do not know when
the time will come.' *Mark 13: 32, 33*

A PRAYER OF PENITENCE

Lord our God,
in our sin we have avoided your call.
Our love for you is like a morning cloud,
like the dew that goes away early.
Have mercy on us;
deliver us from judgement;
bind up our wounds and revive us;
through Jesus Christ our Lord. Amen.

PRAISE

Hills of the north, rejoice,
River and mountain spring
Hark to the advent voice
Valley and lowland, sing
Though absent long, your Lord is nigh;
He judgement brings and victory.

Isles of the southern seas,
Deep in your coral caves,
Pent be each warring breeze
Lulled be your restless waves
He comes to reign with boundless sway,
And make your wastes his great highway.

Lands of the east, awake,
He is your brightest morn,
Greet him with joyous eyes,
Praise shall his path adorn:
The God whom you have longed to know
In Christ draws near, and calls you now.

Shores of the utmost west,
Lands of the setting sun,
Welcome the heavenly guest
In whom the dawn has come:
He brings a never-ending light
Who triumphed o'er our darkest night.

The Word of God

Refrain: PSALM 96
Honour and majesty are before him,
power and splendour in his sanctuary.

9   O worship the Lord in the beauty of holiness;
    let the whole earth tremble before him.
10 Tell it out among the nations that the Lord is king.
    He has made the world so firm that it cannot be
        moved;
    he will judge the peoples with equity.
11 Let the heavens rejoice and let the earth be glad;
    let the sea thunder and all that is in it;
12 Let the fields be joyful and all that is in them;
    let all the trees of the wood shout for joy before
        the Lord.
13 For he comes, he comes to judge the earth;
    with righteousness he will judge the world
        and the peoples with his truth.

A BIBLE READING

Besides this, you know what time it is, how it is now the
moment for you to wake from sleep. For salvation is

nearer to us now than when we became believers; the night is far gone, the day is near. Let us then lay aside the works of darkness and put on the armour of light; let us live honourably as in the day, not in revelling and drunkenness, not in debauchery and licentiousness, not in quarrelling and jealousy. Instead, put on the Lord Jesus Christ, and make no provision for the flesh, to gratify its desires. *Romans 13: 11-13*

Benedictus

1   Blessed be the Lord the God of Israel
     who has come to his people and set them free.

2   The Lord has raised up for us a mighty saviour
     born of the house of his servant David.

3   Through the holy prophets God promised of old
     to save us from our enemies
     from the hands of those who hate us.

4   to show mercy to our forebears
     and to remember his holy covenant.

5   This was the oath God swore to our father Abraham
     to set us free from the hand of our enemies.

6   Free to worship him without fear
     holy and righteous before him all the days of our life.

7   And you child shall be called the prophet of the
       Most High
     for you will go before the Lord to prepare his way.

8   To give his people knowledge of salvation
     by the forgiveness of all their sins.

9   In the tender compassion of our God
     the dawn from on high shall break up on us.

10 To shine on those who dwell in darkness
     and the shadow of death
     and to guide our feet into the way of peace.

Prayer

Pray for
> *the rulers of the world and all who administer*
> *justice,*
> *for people crying for freedom to live as human beings*
> *in peace and dignity,*
> *for all who struggle with sickness, pain and poverty.*

Give thanks for
> *the hope that is ours because of the victory of Christ,*
> *and the assurance that he will judge justly when he*
> *comes again.*

THE COLLECT OF THE DAY

or this prayer:
Almighty God,
Give us grace to cast away the works of darkness
and to put on the armour of light
now in the time of this mortal life in which your Son
Jesus Christ came to us in great humility;
that on the last day
when he shall come again in his glorious majesty
to judge the living and the dead,
we may rise to the life immortal;
through him who is alive and reigns
with you and the Holy Spirit,
one God, now and for ever. Amen.

THE LORD'S PRAYER

AN ENDING

Maranatha. *(An Aramaic word, meaning, O Lord, come.)*
Amen. Even so, come Lord Jesus.

Form 9   The Holy Spirit

Preparation

God's love has been poured into our hearts through the
Holy Spirit that has been given to us. *Romans 5: 5*

Gracious and holy God,
we confess that we have sinned.
Your Spirit gives light, but we have preferred darkness;
your spirit gives wisdom, but we have been foolish;
your spirit gives power, but we have tried to go in our
own strength.
For the sake of Jesus Christ, your Son, forgive our sins,
and enable us by your Spirit to serve you in joyful
obedience,
to the glory of your Name. Amen.

Come, Holy Spirit, souls inspire,
And lighten with celestial fire;
Thou the anointing Spirit art,
Who dost thy seven-fold gifts impart.

Thy blessèd unction from above
Is comfort, life, and fire of love;
Enable with perpetual light
The dulness of our blinded sight.

Anoint and cheer our soilèd face
With the abundance of thy grace;
Keep far our foes, give peace at home:
Where thou art guide no ill can come.

Teach us to know the Father, Son,
And thee, of both, to be but One,
That through the ages all along,
This may be our endless song:

Praise to thy eternal merit,
Father, Son, and Holy Spirit. Amen.

The Word of God

Refrain: PSALM 104

Send your Holy Spirit
and clothe us with power from on high.

26 O Lord, how manifold are your works!
    In wisdom you have made them all;
        the earth is full of your creatures.

27 There is the sea, spread far and wide,
    and there move creatures beyond number,
        both small and great.

28 There go the ships, and there is that Leviathan
    which you have made to play in the deep.

29 All of these look to you
    to give them their food in due season.

30 When you give it them, they gather it;
    you open your hand and they are filled with good.

31 When you hide your face they are troubled;
    when you take away their breath,
        they die and return again to the dust.

32 When you send forth your spirit,
        they are created,
    and you renew the face of the earth.

33 May the glory of the Lord endure for ever;
    may the Lord rejoice in his works;

34 He looks on the earth and it trembles;
   he touches the mountains and they smoke.
35 I will sing to the Lord as long as I live;
   I will make music to my God while I have my
   being.
36 So shall my song please him
   while I rejoice in the Lord.

A BIBLE READING

When the day of Pentecost had come, the disciples
were all together in one place. And suddenly from heaven
there came a sound like the rush of a violent wind,
and it filled the entire house where they were sitting.
Divided tongues, as of fire, appeared among them, and
a tongue rested on each of them. All of them were filled
with the Holy Spirit and began to speak in other languages, as the Spirit gave them ability.

Now there were devout Jews from every nation
under heaven living in Jerusalem. And at this sound
the crowd gathered and was bewildered, because each
one heard them speaking in the native language of
each. Amazed and astonished, they asked, 'Are not all
these who are speaking Galileans? And how is it that
we hear, each of us, in our own native language?
Parthians, Medes, Elamites, and residents of
Mesopotamia, Judea and Cappadocia, Pontus and Asia,
Phrygia and Pamphylia, Egypt and the parts of Libya
belonging to Cyrene, and visitors from Rome, both
Jews and proselytes, Cretans and Arabs in our own languages we hear them speaking about God's deeds of
power.' *Acts 2: 1-11*

Great and Wonderful

1   Great and wonderful are your deeds Lord God, the
        Almighty,
    just and true are your ways, O King of the nations.
2   Who shall not revere and praise your name, O Lord,
    for you alone are holy.
3   All nations shall come and worship in your presence
    for your just dealings have been revealed.
4   To him who sits on the throne, and to the Lamb
    be praise and honour, glory and might,
    for ever and ever. Amen.

Prayer

INTERCESSIONS AND THANKSGIVINGS

Pray for
   the renewal of the church in love and service,
   for the empowering of those called to proclaim
   the mighty works of God,
   for the bestowal of all the gifts of the Spirit
   that people may walk in love, joy and peace.

Give thanks for
   the manifestation of the Spirit's working
   in the lives of men and women,
   for the healing power of the Spirit brings to broken lives.

or this prayer:
Almighty God,
who on the day of Pentecost
sent your Holy Spirit to the apostles
with the wind from heaven and in tongues of flame,
filling them with joy
and boldness to preach the gospel:
By the power of the same Spirit
strengthen us to witness to your truth
and to draw everyone to the fire of your love;
through Jesus Christ our Lord. Amen.

THE LORD'S PRAYER

AN ENDING

The Spirit of truth lead us into all truth,
give us grace to confess that Jesus is Lord
and to proclaim the word and works of God. Amen.

Form 10   The Holy Catholic Church

Preparation

A SENTENCE OF SCRIPTURE

You are the body of Christ and individually members of it. *1 Corinthians 12: 27*

A PRAYER OF PENITENCE

Heavenly Father,
you have called us in your church,
the Body of your Son Jesus Christ,
to continue his work of reconciliation
and reveal you to the world:
but we have failed you, again and again.
Forgive us the sins which continue to tear us apart;
give us the courage to overcome our fears
and to seek that unity which is your gift and your will;
through Jesus Christ our Lord. Amen.

PRAISE

The church's one foundation
Is Jesus Christ her Lord;
She is his new creation
By water and the word:
From heaven he came and sought her
To be his holy Bride;
With his own blood he bought her,
And for her life he died.

Elect from every nation,
Yet one o'er all the earth,
Her charter of salvation
One Lord, one faith, one birth;
One holy Name she blesses,
Partakes one holy food,

And to one hope she presses
With every grace endued.

'Mid toil and tribulation,
And tumult of her war,
She waits the consummation
Of peace for evermore;
Till with the vision glorious
Her longing eyes are blest,
And the great church victorious
Shall be the church at rest.

The Word of God

Refrain:

PSALM 122

We are his people
and the sheep of his pasture.

1   I was glad when they said to me,
    'Let us go to the house of the Lord.'

2   And now our feet are standing
    within your gates, O Jerusalem;

3   Jerusalem, built as a city
    that is at unity in itself.

4   Thither the tribes go up, the tribes of the Lord,
    as is decreed for Israel,
        to give thanks to the name of the Lord.

5   For there are set the thrones of judgement,
    the thrones of the house of David.

6   O pray for the peace of Jerusalem:
    'May they prosper who love you.

7   'Peace be within your walls
    and tranquillity within your palaces.'

8   For my kindred and companions sake,
    I will pray that peace be with you.

9   For the sake of the house of the Lord our God,
    I will seek to do you good.

Come to Christ, a living stone, though rejected by mortals yet chosen and precious in God's sight, and like living stones, let yourselves be built into a spiritual house, to be a holy priesthood, to offer spiritual sacrifices acceptable to God through Jesus Christ. For it stands in scripture:

'See, I am laying in Zion a stone,

a cornerstone chosen and precious;

and whoever believes in him will not be put to shame.'

To you then who believe, he is precious; but for those who do not believe,

'The stone that the builders rejected

has become the very head of the corner,'

and

'A stone that makes them stumble,

and a rock that makes them fall.'

They stumble because they disobey the word, as they were destined to do.

But you are a chosen race, a royal priesthood, a holy nation, God's own people, in order that you may proclaim the mighty acts of him who called you out of darkness into his marvellous light. Once you were not a people, but now you are God's people; once you had not received mercy, but now you have received mercy.

1 Peter 2: 4-10

The Song of Isaiah (Isaiah 12: 2-6)

1   Surely God is my salvation; I will trust, and will not
        be afraid,
        for the Lord God is my strength and my might;
        he has become my salvation.

2   With joy you will draw water:
        from the wells of salvation.

3   And you will say in that day:
        Give thanks to the Lord, call on his name;

4   make known his deeds among the nations;
        proclaim that his name is exalted.

5   Sing praises to the Lord, for he has done gloriously;
        let this be known in all the earth.

6   Shout aloud and sing for joy, O royal Zion,
        for great in your midst is the Holy One of Israel.

Prayer

INTERCESSIONS AND THANKSGIVINGS

Pray for
        the renewal of the church, universal and local,
        the unity of all Christian people, as God wills
        and by the means he chooses,
        the mission and ministries of the church.

Give thanks for
        the apostolic gospel committed to the church,
        the ministry of word, sacrament and prayer,
        the will to unity and its fruit in common action.

or this prayer:

Lord Jesus Christ,
who said to your apostles,
'Peace I leave with you, my peace I give to you':
Look not on our sins but on the faith of your church
and grant it the peace and unity of your kingdom,
where you are alive and reign with the Father
and the Holy Spirit, one God, now and for ever.
Amen

THE LORD'S PRAYER

AN ENDING

To God, who by the power at work within us,
is able to do far more abundantly
than all we ask or think,
to him be glory in the church and in Christ Jesus
to all generations for ever and ever. Amen.
Ephesians 3: 20

Form 11   The Communion of Saints

Preparation

A SENTENCE OF SCRIPTURE

Since we are surrounded by so great a cloud of witness-
es, let us also lay aside every weight and the sin that
clings so closely, and let us run with perseverance the
race that is set before us, looking to Jesus the pioneer
and perfecter of our faith. *Hebrews 12: 1-2*

A PRAYER OF PENITENCE

Lord, you are gracious and compassionate.
Lord, have mercy.

You are loving to all, and your mercy is over all your
creation.
Christ, have mercy.

Your faithful servants bless your name, and speak of
the glory of your kingdom.
Lord, have mercy.

PRAISE

For all the saints, who from their labours rest,
Who thee by faith before the world confessed
Thy Name, O Jesu, be for ever blest. Hallelujah!

O blest communion, fellowship divine!
We feebly struggle, they in glory shine;
And all are one in thee, for all are thine. Hallelujah!

But lo! There breaks a yet more glorious day:
The saints triumphant rise in bright array,
The King of glory passes on his way. Hallelujah!

From earth's wide bounds, from ocean's farthest coast,
Through gates of pearl streams in the countless host,
Singing to Father, Son and Holy Ghost. Hallelujah!

The Word of God

Refrain:

Bring us with your saints,
to glory everlasting.

1   Alleluia. O sing to the Lord a new song;
       sing his praise in the congregation of the faithful.

2   Let Israel rejoice in their maker;
       let the children of Zion be joyful in their king.

3   Let them praise his name in the dance;
       let them sing praise to him with timbrel and lyre.

4   For the Lord has pleasure in his people
       and adorns the poor with salvation.

5   Let the faithful be joyful in glory;
       let them rejoice in their ranks, Alleluia.

A BIBLE READING

After this I, John, looked, and there was a great mult-
itude that no one could count, from every nation, from
all tribes and peoples and languages, standing before
the throne and before the Lamb, robed in white, with
palm branches in their hands. They cried out in a loud
voice, saying, 'Salvation belongs to our God who is seated on the throne, and to the Lamb!' And all the angels
stood around the throne and around the elders and the
four living creatures, and they fell on their faces before
the throne and worshipped God, singing, 'Amen!
Blessing and glory and wisdom and thanksgiving and
honour and power and might be to our God for ever
and ever! Amen.' Then one of the elders said to me,
'These are they who have come out of the great ordeal;
they have washed their robes and made them white in
the blood of the Lamb. For this reason they are before
the throne of God, and worship him day and night

within his temple, and the one who is seated on the throne will shelter them. They will hunger no more, and thirst no more; the sun will not strike them, nor any scorching heat; for the Lamb at the centre of the throne will be their shepherd, and he will guide them to springs of the water of life, and God will wipe away every tear from their eyes.' *Revelation 7: 9-12, 14-17*

Glory and Honour

1   Glory and honour and power
    are yours by right, O Lord our God.

2   For you created all things
    and by your will they have their being.

3   Glory and honour and power
    are yours by right, O Lamb for us slain;

4   For by your blood you ransomed us for God
    from every race and language
        from every people and nation.

5   To make us a kingdom of priests
    to stand and serve before our God.

6   To him who sits on the throne and to the Lamb
    be praise and honour glory and might
        for ever and ever. Amen.

Prayer

INTERCESSIONS AND THANKSGIVINGS

Give thanks for the triumphs of the gospel that herald your salvation,

the human lives that reveal your work of grace,
the unceasing praise of the company of heaven.

Pray for grace to live as those who believe in the communion of saints,

and for all who mourn.

or this prayer:

Almighty and eternal God,
you have kindled the flame of love
in the hearts of the saints:
Grant to us the same faith and power of love,
that, as we rejoice in their triumphs,
we may be sustained by their example and fellowship;
through Jesus Christ our Lord.

THE LORD'S PRAYER

AN ENDING

May we live by faith, walk in hope
and be renewed in love,
until the world reflects your glory
and you are all in all.
Even so, come Lord Jesus. Amen.

Form 12   Resurrection of the Body and the Life Everlasting

Preparation

Our citizenship is in heaven. And we eagerly await a Saviour from there, the Lord Jesus Christ, who, by the power that enables him to bring everything under his control, will transform our lowly bodies so that they will be like his glorious body.

Philippians 3: 20, 21 (TNIV)

A PRAYER OF PENITENCE

God of mercy,
we acknowledge that we are all sinners.
We turn from the wrong things
we have thought and said and done,
and remember all that we have failed to do.
For the sake of Jesus, who died for us,
forgive what is past,
and help us to live each day as if it might be our last;
through Jesus Christ our Lord. Amen.

PRAISE

Abide with me, fast falls the eventide;
The darkness deepens, Lord, with me abide;
When other helpers fail and comforts flee,
Help of the helpless, O abide with me.

Swift to its close ebbs out life's little day;
Earth's joys grow dim, its glories pass away;
Change and decay in all around I see;
O thou who changest not, abide with me.

I fear no foe with thee at hand to bless;
Ills have no weight, and tears no bitterness.

Where is death's sting? Where, grave, thy victory?
I triumph still, if thou abide with me.

Hold thou thy Cross before my closing eyes;
Shine through the gloom, and point me to the skies,
Heaven's morning breaks, and earth's vain shadows flee;
In life, in death, O Lord, abide with me.

The Word of God

PSALM 121

Refrain:
Goodness and mercy shall follow me
all the days of my life.

1   I lift up my eyes hills;
     from where is my help to come?
2   My help comes from the Lord,
     the maker of heaven and earth.
3   He will not suffer your foot to stuble;
     he who watches over you will not sleep.
4   Behold, he who keeps watch over Israel
     shall neither slumber nor sleep.
5   The Lord himself watches over you;
     the Lord is your shade at your right hand,
6   So that the sun shall not strike you by day,
     neither the moon by night.
7   The Lord shall keep you from all evil;
     it is he who shall keep your soul.
8   The Lord shall keep watch over your going out
        and your coming in,
     from this time forth for evermore.

A BIBLE READING

Jesus said, 'Do not let your hearts be troubled. Believe
in God, believe also in me. In my Father's house there
are many dwelling places. If it were not so, would I

have told you that I go to prepare a place for you? And if I go and prepare a place for you, I will come again and will take you to myself, so that where I am, there you may be also. And you know the way to the place where I am going.' Thomas said to him, 'Lord, we do not know where you are going. How can we know the way?' Jesus said to him, 'I am the way, and the truth, and the life. No one comes to the Father except through me.'

'Peace I leave with you; my peace I give to you. I do not give as the world gives. Do not let your hearts be troubled and do not let them be afraid.'
John 14: 1-6, 27

Nunc Dimittis (Luke 2: 29-32)

1   Now, Lord, you let your servant go in peace;
    your word has been fulfilled.

2   My own eyes have seen the salvation
    which you have prepared in the sight of every people.

3   A light to reveal you to the nations,
    and the glory of your people Israel.

Prayer

INTERCESSIONS AND THANKSGIVINGS

Pray for the a renewal of faith,
   for the dying and those who mourn,
   for ministries of care and healing.

Give thanks for all those who have died in the faith of Christ,
   for the promise to those who mourn that all tears
      shall be wiped away,
   for the pledge of death destroyed and victory won.

or this prayer:

Heavenly Father, in your Son Jesus Christ you have given us a true faith and a sure hope. Strengthen this faith and hope in us all our days, that we may live as those who believe in the communion of saints, the forgiveness of sin, and the resurrection to eternal life; through Jesus Christ our Lord. Amen.

THE LORD'S PRAYER

AN ENDING

Heavenly Father:
In darkness and in light,
in trouble and in joy,
help us to trust your love,
to serve your purpose
and to praise your name;
through Jesus Christ our Lord. Amen.

or

May God in his infinite love and mercy
bring the whole church,
living and departed in the Lord Jesus,
to a joyful resurrection
and the fulfilment of his eternal kingdom. Amen

Form 13   The Saints of Ireland

Preparation

Look to the rock from which you were hewn, and to the
quarry from which you were dug. *Isaiah 51: 1*

A PRAYER OF PENITENCE

O taste and see that the Lord is good.
Happy are those who trust in him.
Lord, have mercy.

The Lord ransoms the lives of his servants
and none who trust in him will be destroyed.
Christ, have mercy.

Come my children, listen to me;
I will teach you the fear of the Lord.
Lord, have mercy.

PRAISE

It were my soul's desire
To see the face of God;
It were my soul's desire
To rest in his abode.

Grant, Lord, my soul's desire
Deep waves of cleansing sighs.
Grant, Lord, my soul's desire
From earthly cares to rise.

It were my soul's desire
To imitate my king.
It were my soul's desire
His endless praise to bring.

This still my soul's desire
Whatever life afford,

To gain my soul's desire
And see thy face, O Lord.

The Word of God

Refrain: PSALM 125

Your fame reached to far-off islands,
and you were loved for your peaceful reign.

1   Those who trust in the Lord are like Mount Zion,
    which cannot be moved, but stands fast for ever.
2   As the hills stand about Jerusalem,
    so the Lord stands round about his people,
        from this time forth for evermore.
3   The sceptre of wickedness shall not hold sway
        over the land allotted to the righteous,
    lest the righteous turn their hands to evil.
4   Do good, O Lord, to those who are good,
    and to those who are true of heart.
5   Those who turn aside to crooked ways the Lord
    shall take away with the evildoers;
    but let there be peace upon Israel.

A BIBLE READING

Jesus said to his disciples; 'Go therefore and make disciples of all nations, baptizing them in the name of the Father and of the Son and of the Holy Spirit, and teaching them to obey everything that I have commanded you. And remember, I am with you always, to the end of the age.' *Matthew 28: 19-20*

A CANTICLE

A Song of Saint Patrick
I bind unto myself today
The strong Name of the Trinity,
By invocation of the same,
The Three in One and One in Three.

I bind this day to me for ever,
By pow'r of faith, Christ's incarnation;
His baptism in Jordan river;
His death on Cross for my salvation;
His bursting from the spiced tomb;
His riding up the heav'nly way;
His coming at the day of doom;
I bind unto myself today.

Christ be with me, Christ within me,
Christ behind me, Christ before me,
Christ beside me, Christ to win me,
Christ to comfort and restore me,
Christ beneath me, Christ above me,
Christ in quiet, Christ in danger,
Christ in hearts of all that love me,
Christ in mouth of friend and stranger.

I bind unto myself today
The strong Name of the Trinity,
By invocation of the same,
The Three in One and One in Three.
Of whom all nature hath creation;
Eternal Father, Spirit, Word:
Praise to the Lord of my salvation,
Salvation is of Christ the Lord. Amen.

Prayer

INTERCESSIONS AND THANKSGIVINGS

*Give thanks for those who first proclaimed the gospel in
Ireland:*

> *Patrick, Ailbhe and Brigid,*
> *for those who taught the Christian Faith and laid the
> foundations:*
> *Finnian, Comgall, Munchin and Finbarre,*

for those who went forth from Ireland in the service
of the gospel:
Columba, Columbanus, Gall, Brendan and
Charles Inglis,
for reformers and rebuilders:
Malachy, Richard FitzRalph, Jeremy Taylor.

Pray that what is amiss today may be corrected
and what is lacking may be supplied,
that we may more and more bring forth fruit to the
glory of God.

THE COLLECT OF THE DAY

or this prayer:
Hear us, most merciful God,
for that part of the church
which you planted in this island.
May it hold fast the faith which you gave to the saints
and live in the love that, shining through them,
made them lights in the darkness of their times,
and so shall it bear much fruit to eternal life;
through Jesus Christ our Lord. Amen.

THE LORD'S PRAYER

AN ENDING

Let us go forth,
in the goodness of our merciful Father,
in the gentleness of Jesus our brother,
in the radiance of the Holy Spirit,
in the faith of the apostles,
in the holiness of the saints,
in the courage of the martyrs. Amen.

Form 14   The Holy Communion

May be used on a Saturday in preparation for communion

Preparation

As often as you eat this bread and drink the cup, you
proclaim the Lord's death until he comes.
1 Corinthians 11: 26

I confess to God Almighty,
the Father, the Son, and the Holy Spirit,
before the whole company of heaven,
that I have sinned in thought, word, and deed,
through my own grievous fault.
Wherefore I pray God to have mercy upon me.
Almighty God, have mercy upon me,
forgive me all my sins,
deliver me from all evil,
confirm and strengthen me in all goodness,
and bring me to life everlasting;
through Jesus Christ our Lord. Amen.

Jesu, thou joy of loving hearts;
Thou Fount of life, thou Light of men;
From the best bliss that earth imparts
We turn unfilled to thee again.

Thy truth unchanged hath ever stood;
Thou savest those that on thee call;
To them that seek thee, thou art good,
To them that find thee, all in all.

We taste thee, O thou living Bread,
And long to feast upon thee still;
We drink of thee, the Fountain-head,
And thirst our souls from thee to fill.

O Jesus, ever with us stay,
Make all our moments calm and bright,
Chase the dark night of sin away,
Shed o'er the world thy holy light.

The Word of God

PSALM 116

Refrain:
I will go to the altar of God
to the God of my joy and gladness.

10 How shall I repay the Lord
 for all the benefits he has given to me?

11 I will lift up the cup of salvation
 and call upon the name of the Lord.

12 I will fulfil my vows to the Lord
 in the presence of all his people.

15 I will offer to you a sacrifice of thanksgiving
 and call upon the name of the Lord.

16 I will fulfil my vows to the Lord
 in the presence of all his people,

17 In the courts of the house of the Lord,
 in the midst of you, O Jerusalem. Alleluia.

A BIBLE READING

Jesus said, 'I am the bread of life. Whoever comes to me
will never be hungry, and whoever believes in me will
never be thirsty.' He also said, 'Very truly, I tell you,
unless you eat the flesh of the Son of Man and drink his
blood, you have no life in you. Those who eat my flesh
and drink my blood have eternal life, and I will raise

them up on the last day; for my flesh is true food and my
blood is true drink. Those who eat my flesh and drink my
blood abide in me, and I in them.' *John 6: 35, 53-56*

The Easter Anthems

1 Christ our passover has been sacrificed for us:
   therefore let us celebrate the feast.

2 Not with the old leaven of corruption and wickedness
   but with the unleavened bread of sincerity and truth.

3 Christ once raised from the dead dies no more:
   death has no more dominion over him.

4 In dying he died to sin once for all:
   in living he lives to God.

5 See yourselves therefore as dead to sin:
   and alive to God in Jesus Christ our Lord.

6 Christ has been raised from the dead:
   the first fruits of those who sleep.

7 For as by man came death:
   by man has come also the resurrection of the dead.

8 For as in Adam all die:
   even so in Christ shall all be made alive.

Prayer

INTERCESSIONS AND THANKSGIVINGS

Give thanks for the gift of the sacrament of the Lord's Supper,
*   by which we are spiritually fed with the Body and*
*   Blood of Christ,*
*   for particular things for which we will give thanks*
*   at the eucharist.*

Pray that the souls of all who share in Holy Communion
*   may be strengthened and refreshed;*
*   for ... to be remembered before God,*
*   individuals or causes for which we shall especially*
*   pray.*

Form 14   65

Lord Jesus Christ,
in a wonderful sacrament
you have given us a memorial of your passion:
grant us so to reverence the sacred mysteries
of your body and blood
that we may know within ourselves
the fruit of your redemption,
for you are alive and reign
with the Father and the Holy Spirit,
one God, now and for ever.

or this prayer:
Father, we were not fit
even to eat the crumbs from under your table.
But you, Lord, are the God of our salvation,
and share your bread with sinners.
So cleanse and feed us
with the precious body and blood of your Son,
that he may live in us and we in him;
and that we, with the whole company of Christ,
may sit and eat in your kingdom. Amen.

THE LORD'S PRAYER

AN ENDING

Abide with us, Lord Jesus,
for the night is at hand and the day is far spent.
As the night watch looks for the morning,
so do we long for you, O Christ.
Come then with the dawning (or in the fulness) of the
new day,
and make yourself known to us
in the breaking of the bread. Amen.

or
The Lord bless us and watch over us,
make his face shine on us and be gracious to us,
and give us his peace. Amen.

Form 15   In sickness and in health

Preparation

You shall not be afraid of any terror by night, nor the arrow that flies by day; of the pestilence that stalks in darkness, nor of the sickness that destroys at noonday. *Psalm 91: 5,6*

A PRAYER OF PENITENCE

Father, you are the source of all health:
Lord, have mercy.

Lord Jesus, you heal the sick and forgive sinners:
Christ, have mercy.

Holy Spirit, from whom come healing and comfort:
Lord, have mercy..

PRAISE

My song is love unknown,
My Saviour's love to me,
Love to the loveless shown,
That they might lovely be.
O who am I,
That for my sake
My Lord should take
Frail flesh and die?

He came from his blest throne,
Salvation to bestow;
But men made strange, and none
The longed-for Christ would know.
But O, my Friend,
My Friend indeed,
Who at my need
His life did spend.

Here might I stay and sing,
No story so divine;
Never was love, dear King,
Never was grief like thine!
This is my friend
In whose sweet praise
I all my days
Could gladly spend.

The Word of God

Refrain PSALM 46

On God alone my soul in stillness waits;
from him comes my salvation.

1   God is our refuge and strength,
      a very present help in trouble;

2   Therefore we will not fear, though the earth be
      moved,
      and though the mountains tremble in the heart
      of the sea;

3   Though the waters rage and swell,
      and though the mountains quake at the towering
         seas.

4   There is a river whose streams make glad the city
         of God,
      the holy place of the dwelling of the Most High.

5   God is in the midst of her;
         therefore shall she not be removed;
      God shall help her at the break of day.

6   The nations are in uproar and the kingdoms are
         shaken,
      but God utters his voice and the earth shall melt
         away.

7   The Lord of hosts is with us;
      the God of Jacob is our stronghold.

8   Come and behold the works of the Lord,
    what destruction he has wrought upon the earth.

9   He makes wars to cease in all the world;
    he shatters the bow and snaps the spear
    and burns the chariots in the fire.

10 'Be still, and know that I am God;
    I will be exalted among the nations;
    I will be exalted in the earth.'

11 The Lord of hosts is with us;
    the God of Jacob is our stronghold.

A BIBLE READING

He was despised and rejected by others;
    a man of suffering and acquainted with infirmity;
and as one from whom others hide their faces
    he was despised, and we held him of no account.
Surely he has borne our infirmities
    and carried our diseases;
yet we accounted him stricken,
    struck down by God, and afflicted.
But he was wounded for our transgressions,
    crushed for our iniquities;
upon him was the punishment that made us whole,
    and by his bruises we are healed.
All we like sheep have gone astray;
    we have all turned to our own way,
and the Lord has laid on him
    the iniquity of us all. *Isaiah 53: 3-6*

Saviour of the World

1   Jesus Saviour of the world, come to us in your mercy:
    we look to you to save and help us.

2   By your cross and your life laid down, you set
            your people free:
    we look to you to save and help us.

3   When they were ready to perish you saved your
            disciples:
    we look to you to come to our help.

4   In the greatness of your mercy loose us from
            our chains:
    forgive the sins of all your people.

5   Make yourself known as our Saviour and mighty
            Deliverer:
    save and help us that we may praise you.

6   Come now and dwell with us Lord Christ Jesus,
    hear our prayer and be with us always.

7   And when you come in your glory
    make us to be one with you
    and to share the life of your kingdom. Amen.

Prayer   INTERCESSIONS AND THANKSGIVINGS

Give thanks for

> the gift of health and gifts of healings,
> the skills of surgeons, doctors, nurses and therapists,
> particular blessings received.

Pray

> that those who are sick may be receive healing
>   and refreshment of spirt,
> that cures may be discovered for illnesses which at
>   present seem to have no cure,
> for all who are anxious about loved ones or who fear
>   an uncertain future.

Almighty God,
your blessed Son went about doing and healing all
manner of sickness:
Continue his gracious work among us
(especially in hospitals and nursing-homes);
cheer, heal and sanctify all who are sick;
to all in the healing professions grant wisdom and
skill, sympathy and patience;
and pour out your blessing on all who seek to relieve
suffering and forward your purposes of love;
through Jesus Christ our Lord.

THE LORD'S PRAYER

AN ENDING

The Lord bless us and watch over us,
make his face shine on us and be gracious to us,
and give us his peace.

The Lord's Prayer

Our Father in heaven,
    hallowed be your name,
    your kingdom come,
    your will be done,
        on earth as in heaven.
Give us today our daily bread.
Forgive us our sins
    as we forgive those who sin against us.
Lead us not into temptation,
    but deliver us from evil.
For the kingdom, the power, and the glory are yours
    now and for ever. Amen.

or

Our Father, who art in heaven,
    hallowed be thy name,
    thy kingdom come,
    thy will be done,
        on earth as it is in heaven.
Give us this day our daily bread.
And forgive us our trespasses
    as we forgive those who trespass against us.
And lead us not into temptation
    but deliver us from evil.
For thine is the kingdom the power and the glory
    for ever and ever. Amen.

Acknowledgements

Texts are reproduced with the permission of the copyright owners from:

The Book of Common Prayer of the Church of Ireland (Revision of 2004) © 2003 Representative Church Body, Church of Ireland House, Dublin 6.

Bible passages are from the *New Revised Standard Version*, Anglicized edition, © 1989, 1995 by the Division of Christian Education of the National Council of Churches of Christ in the USA, and are used by permission. All rights reserved.

The sentence in Form 12 is from *Today's New International Version* (TNIV) © 2002 by the International Bible Society. Used by permission of Hodder and Stoughton Publishers. All rights reserved.

Psalms are from the Psalter in *Common Worship: Services and Prayers for the Church of England* © 2000 by Archbishops' Council. The collects in Forms 4 and 6 are also from *Common Worship*. The shorter ending in Form 12 is from *Common Worship: Pastoral Services*. The prayer of penitence in Form 8 is from *New Patterns of Worship* © 2002 Archbishops' Council.

The canticles in Forms 1, 3, 4, 8 and 12 are © 1988 English Language Liturgical Consultation (ELLC).

The ending in Form 13 is from a prayer by David Adam © 1998.

The prayer of penitence in Form 7 is adapted from a prayer in the *Book of Common Worship* of the Presbyterian Church in the USA, © 1993 Westminster/John Knox Press.

The prayer of penitence in Form 9 is adapted from a prayer in the *Methodist Worship Book*, © 1999 Trustees for Methodist Church Purposes.